Sandi Toksvig's
GUIDE TO FRANCE

This activity book belongs to:

....

RED FOX

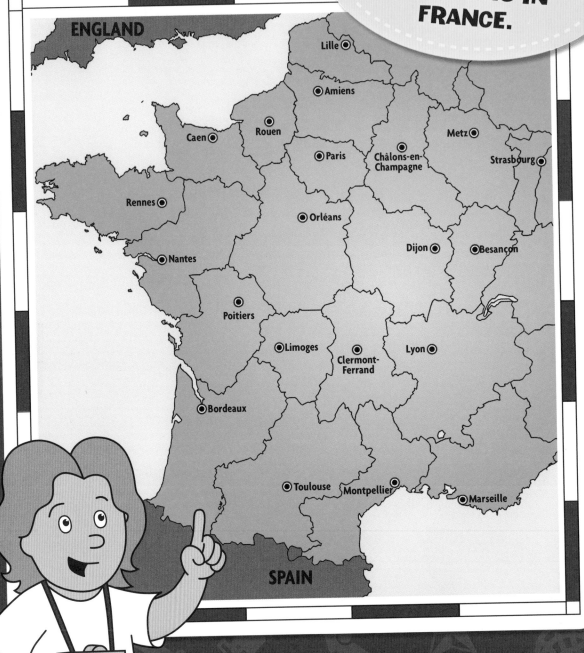

DRAW A CIRCLE ON THE MAP WHERE YOU ARE GOING IN FRANCE.

Population: About 60 million

Language: French (obviously)

Size: 211,209 miles² (547,030 km²)

Coastline: 3,844 miles (6,186 km)

Capital City: Paris

Population of Paris: About 2.15 million

Currency: Euro (€). There are 100 cents in 1 Euro

Welcome to France (Bienvenue en France)

There is so much to see and do in France! This guide will help you to remember where you went and what you did. You can even learn how to say things in French, and there are games and activities just to make sure you never get bored. I'll also tell you some quite interesting things about the country and the people who live there.

Did you know that France is the largest country in Western Europe? This is a good thing because it is the most visited country in the world, so they need the space! 79 million tourists visit each year (and you thought you were the only one). That's a lot of people!

France has every kind of landscape you can imagine. There are really old mountain ranges like the Massif Central and the Ardennes, which are about a billion years old, and then there are younger mountains like the Pyrenees and the Alps, which are only about 30 million years old. It has famous buildings you will have heard of like the Eiffel Tower, as well as great places to swim and go skiing. One of the 10 Disneylands in the world is near Paris.

I'm sure you'll see masses of exciting things during your stay and have lots of fun. Make sure you write them all down in this book. Now, follow me and let's find out more about France!

Sandi Toksvig

GETTING PLACES

There are lots of different ways to get to France, and the cities and villages there. How did you travel?

By Plane

There are around 478 airports in France if you count the smaller ones. The biggest airport is Charles de Gaulle International just outside Paris. The French national airline is Air France.

⩨ CURIOUS FACT ⩨

Most people agree that the first time humans managed to fly was in Paris in 1783. Two men went 5 miles (8 km) in a hot-air balloon. The only problem? The balloon was powered by a wood fire, and had no steering. It went wherever the wind took it, which would be no good if you had an appointment.

By Boat

France has 10 major ports. The largest is Marseille. Once you get here there are a further 9,278 miles (14,932 km) of waterways running across the country.

The Millau Viaduct

By Road

There's about 555,070 miles (893,300 km) of road in France, so don't think you'll cover all of it if you're travelling by car. The national cars are Renault, Peugeot and Citroën. See if you can spot some. France has the world's tallest road bridge, which is called the Millau Viaduct. It was opened in 2004.

By Train

France has more railway than any other country in Western Europe. 19,784 miles (31,840 km) to be exact. They have brilliant high-speed trains like the TGV, which can do 200 miles (320 km) per hour. That's very fast! Using the Channel Tunnel, a Eurostar train can travel from London to Paris in about two hours.

Through the Channel Tunnel

The Channel Tunnel opened in 1994 and is the longest undersea tunnel in the world. The official border between France and the United Kingdom is marked by a stainless-steel band, roughly halfway along the tunnel.

FACTS ABOUT THE TUNNEL

- It is 31.35 miles (50.45 km) long and connects Folkestone, England, to Coquelles in northern France.
- It is the second-longest rail tunnel in the world.
- At its deepest point it is 60 metres (197 feet) beneath the seabed.

≹ CURIOUS FACT ≹

It was a French engineer, Albert Mathieu-Favier, who first suggested the idea of a tunnel in 1802. Back then it would have cost £1 million. Travel would have been by horse-drawn coaches. The idea was to have an island in the middle where the horses could get some air. The final cost of the actual tunnel was £10 billion (with no horses and no island).

TRAVEL GAMES
Travelling can be a bit boring sometimes!
Here are some games that might be fun...

COUNTING COWS

This game does not work well in the city. It is played by two people on opposite sides of a car. Each person counts how many cows they see on their side, and each cow is one point. If, however, side A passes a cemetery on their side, then side B shouts, 'Your cows are buried!' and side A loses all their points. A white horse counts as a bonus of 10 points. The person with the most points at the end of the car journey wins.

TRAVEL BINGO

Make some bingo cards before you go with things you might see on the way. The first person to tick off everything on their card wins.

Here are some ideas to get you started
(see you if you can say them in French too):

Bakery	Florist	Church	Supermarket
boulangerie	*fleuriste*	*église*	*supermarché*
Cyclist	School	Someone talking on the phone	Statue of a horse
cycliste	*école*	*quelqu'un qui est au téléphone*	*statue d'un cheval*

YOUR TICKET

Stick your train, plane or boat ticket here!

Windy Noises! (NB: Don't read this. It is very rude.)

Try to think of the worst person you could be sharing your trip with. I would not have wanted to travel with a Frenchman called Le Pétomane.

Sometimes when you are travelling in a car or small space there can be a problem with someone being a bit . . . well . . . windy. The person may allow small noises to escape, which may make a smell. The French call this to *péter*. There was a French entertainer called Joseph Pujol (1857–1945) who was so good at *péter*-ing that he made money from it.

But he didn't make just any noises – sometimes they sounded like musical instruments! He could also make the sound of cannon fire, thunderstorms and *péter* the whole of the French national anthem. He became a great star, but you probably wouldn't want to travel with him!

FRENCH FACTS

Officially France is called the French Republic.

The French flag is called *le drapeau tricolore* (which just means three-coloured flag – see, French is not that difficult). It is blue, white and red. Can you see any French flags where you are staying?

The National Anthem

The French national anthem is the *La Marseillaise* or 'song from Marseille'. It's a great tune although the words are not very friendly because there is a lot of talk about blood and killing. Maybe if you ask nicely a French person you meet might sing it to you!

Houses

If you lived in France you'd probably live in a town or city. Only 25% of French people live in the countryside.

Money

The French once used the Franc but they now have the Euro. There are 100 cents in 1 Euro.

The sign for the Euro looks like this:

Try to get a cent coin and stick it here. (Don't do this if you are hungry and it's the last one you've got.)

Entertainment

There are six French television channels. Did you know that the French read more magazines than anybody else in the world?

Find a French newspaper or magazine and write the name here:

Where I Stayed

Depending what kind of holiday you are taking, you could be staying in all sorts of different places. It might be a tent, caravan, hotel, ski chalet or house.

I am staying . . .

I like it because . . .

Things that are close to where I am staying include . . .

Draw a picture here of what you can see from your bedroom window (or outside your tent!):

WHAT'S DIFFERENT ABOUT FRANCE?

There are some things that might be different when you're on holiday in France:

• In France they drive on the right-hand side of the road, so be very careful near traffic and make sure you look in all directions when you cross.

• Not everyone speaks English. Try to speak some French. Even if you can just say one word! Maybe you could learn how to ask someone if they speak English: *Parlez-vous anglais?* You might have to practise this a few times but don't give up. Ask the adult who you are with for some help.

• Remember to say *Bonjour* when you meet someone, even a shopkeeper. Look at pages 17–21 for some other words.

• Don't be surprised if a French person you've met before gives you *la bise*. This is not a rude thing. It's a kiss on each cheek.

BONJOUR!

• Make sure you ask if you would like ice in your drink, otherwise you might not get any.

• French people like to have a big lunch and a smaller dinner. In many places the shops are closed in the afternoons so that everyone can relax after their lunch – they might even have a quick nap!

SPOT THE DIFFERENCE

Look carefully at these two pictures of me at a French café. Can you spot the differences? Circle them in picture B. There are 10 things to find.

FRENCH HOLIDAYS

The French like to enjoy life and they have 11 public holidays. You may be visiting during one of these celebrations. The biggest ones are:

New Year's Day - Le jour de l'an

This is on 1 January, like many other countries in the world.

Labour Day - La fête du travail

This is on 1 May. People often pick wild Lily of the Valley (*le muguet*) flowers. You may see the flowers being sold by the side of the road or to make money for charity.

Bastille Day - La fête nationale

14 July is France's national day. They call it *le quatorze juillet*. It is the British who call it Bastille Day, which refers to when the French got rid of their royal family. But actually it was designed to celebrate the royals. King Louis XVI (who was later guillotined) himself took part in the first celebrations.

Christmas - Noël

25 December. Christmas is an important holiday. A typical Christmas meal might include a *Bûche de Noël*, a traditional French Christmas cake that looks like a log. Most families will open their presents on Christmas Eve rather than Christmas Day. Lots of people go to church at midnight on Christmas Eve, then they have the *Réveillon*, a huge late-night feast sometimes followed by a *mal de tête* (a headache).

School holidays - Les vacances scolaires

France is divided into three school zones. They often holiday at different times so that the ski slopes and beaches don't get too crowded. There are five school holiday periods: *La Toussaint* (All Saints' Day), *Noël* (Christmas), *Hiver* (Winter), *Printemps* (Spring) and *Été* (Summer). Some schools only have a four-day week with no school on Wednesdays and weekends.

JOURNAL

Holidays are usually so busy with lots going on that when you get home you've forgotten what happened! Use these pages to write a journal about the places you visited and the things you did.

JOURNAL

PARIS

Hmm, where to begin? It's the capital of France. About two million people live there and it's a pretty old place! Paris is the most popular tourist destination in the world – 30 million foreign visitors turn up each year. If you go there on holiday there is lots to do.

Geography: The River Seine runs through Paris. Paris has two islands and a few hills – the highest is Montmartre at 130 metres (426 feet). There is also a 'left bank' and a 'right bank' of the River Seine, as sometimes it's hard to know where you are because the river curves so much.

Stuff you have to see (or at least tell people you've seen and buy a postcard...):

The Eiffel Tower: You probably already know what this looks like. It is one of the most recognized pieces of metal in the world and probably the most visited monument anywhere.

It's quite difficult to miss as it's the tallest thing in Paris (324 metres or 1,063 feet, about the height of a building with 81 floors). The view from the top is fantastic but almost seven million people visit each year (that makes about 200,000,000 since it opened) so don't expect to have the place to yourself. If you are there in the winter you can go ice skating for free on the first floor.

CURIOUS FACTS

- *The tower weighs 7,300 tons. That's about 1,500 elephants.*

- *It was made with 18,038 pieces of iron and 2.5 million rivets. If you laid all the iron pieces end to end the tower would fall down.*

- *If there is a high wind don't think you are going crazy when you feel the tower sway 5–10 centimetres.*

Notre Dame de Paris

A twelfth-century cathedral on the Île de la Cité island. It is where the Hunchback of Notre Dame was supposed to live. Imagine building this huge place before there were cranes, steel or computers to tell you if it was all going to stand up when it was finished!

The Louvre

The Louvre art gallery has so much stuff that I once found a painting I was looking for outside the ladies' toilets! Either decide exactly what you want to see or just wander about and make discoveries like:

CURIOUS FACT:
Venus has no arms

- **The Venus de Milo statue**
- **The Mona Lisa**
- **The Egyptian collection**

CURIOUS FACT:
Mona Lisa has no eyebrows

Le Centre Georges Pompidou, also known as Beaubourg

This place looks great even from the outside. All the pipes for the building are outside and painted bright colours. There is also a Children's Gallery (*Galerie des enfants*) with special exhibits just for kids.

The Sewers (Les égouts)

This is the place to go if you want to find out what happens to stuff when you flush the toilet! Paris has over 1,491 miles (2,400 km) of underground passageways for sewage. You can go on a guided tour but I wouldn't suggest bringing back any souvenirs. (P.S. Don't wear your best shoes.)

Le Bois de Boulogne

A 2,000-acre park with loads to do. You can rent bikes, row boats, play mini golf and check out the *Jardin d'Acclimatation*. It's a park just for kids that includes a science museum and puppet shows.

Le Parc de la Villette

The biggest park in Paris. Quite often in the summer there are street performers here. There are 11 different gardens, with three especially for kids.

True or False?

During the First World War, parrots were kept on the top of the Eiffel Tower to warn about enemy planes.

True! Parrots have excellent hearing and would begin to squawk when they heard planes long before humans had any idea that something was coming

SPEAKING IN FRENCH

The fun thing about going to France is that you can learn to say some words in French, and have fun working out what different things mean (like signs and menus). 200 million people in the world, many of them children, speak French, so it can't be that difficult.

Basically, the way it works is that *cheval* means 'horse' and it's like that the whole way through – they have a different word for each one of ours. Of course, there are exceptions like *le week-end* – which means 'the weekend', and *le pique-nique*, which means . . . well, I think you've got the hang of it!

FACT:
Did you know that French was the official language of England for over 300 years?

Here are some words that are really useful to know. Take this guide out with you so you can practise. Ask an adult to help you learn how to say the words.

One	*Un*	**Yes**	*Oui*
Two	*Deux*	**No**	*Non*
Three	*Trois*	**Please**	*S'il vous plaît*
Four	*Quatre*	**Thank you**	*Merci*
Five	*Cinq*	**Monday**	*Lundi*
Six	*Six*	**Tuesday**	*Mardi*
Seven	*Sept*	**Wednesday**	*Mercredi*
Eight	*Huit*	**Thursday**	*Jeudi*
Nine	*Neuf*	**Friday**	*Vendredi*
Ten	*Dix*	**Saturday**	*Samedi*
Fifty	*Cinquante*	**Sunday**	*Dimanche*
One hundred	*Cent*	**Chocolate**	*Chocolat*

COUNTING IN FRENCH

Look at the picture below and the items underneath.
How many of each of the items can you see in the picture?
Write the number in French (clue: look at the list of numbers on page 17).

PHRASES TO USE

These are some simple phrases that you might want to get the hang of on holiday. Ask an adult to help you learn how to say the words.

The main thing to remember, when speaking French is to shift your shoulders, wave your hands and loosen your lips. The French move everything when they speak. If you don't know a word, try taking the English word and making it sound French, like:

tourist information = *information touristique*

passport = *passeport*

FACT:
The phone number for the emergency services in France is 112

My name is _____	*Je m'appelle* _____
I come from Britain	*Je suis britannique*
Where is _____ ?	*Où est* _____ ?
I am on holiday	*Je suis en vacances*
I would like _____	*Je voudrais* _____
How much does _____ **cost?**	*Combien ça coûte* _____ ?
Open	*Ouvert*
Closed	*Fermé*
Sweets	*Bonbons*

What floor are we on?

Ground floor	*Rez-de-chaussée*
First floor	*Premier étage*
Second floor	*Deuxième étage*

After that just keep counting, but do take the lift.

Some phrases I hope you won't need:

I'm lost	*Je suis perdu*
Help!	*Au secours!*

Once you've learned how to say some simple words, here are some more important phrases to annoy adults with:

Are we nearly there?

Est-ce que nous sommes presque arrivés?

You're supposed to drive on the right.

Tu es censé conduire à droite.

Your suitcase is stuck on the conveyor belt.

Ta valise est bloquée sur le tapis roulant.

There's no toilet paper.

Il n'y a pas de papier toilette.

Just one more ride, please.

Encore un tour, s'il te plaît.

FACT:
What's the first word in the French language?
à, meaning
'to' or 'at'.

Le pot d'échappement est tombé.

The exhaust pipe has fallen off.

Je suis désolé, il n'aurait pas dû faire ça.

I'm very sorry, he shouldn't have done that.

Tout le monde te regarde.

Everyone is looking at you.

FACT:
What French word
has all five vowels
in it?

Oiseau – 'bird'

DICTIONARY

apple	*pomme*		**I'm hungry**	*j'ai faim*
airport	*aéroport*		**juice**	*jus*
banana	*banane*		**lunch**	*déjeuner*
beach	*plage*		**mother**	*mère*
bicycle	*bicyclette*		**orange**	*orange*
boat	*bâteau*		**plane**	*avion*
breakfast	*petit déjeuner*		**sandwich**	*sandwich*
brother	*frère*		**sister**	*sœur*
car	*voiture*		**skis**	*skis*
caravan	*caravane*		**snowboard**	*snowboard*
cheese	*fromage*		**sunglasses**	*lunettes de soleil*
cold	*froid*		**sunscreen**	*crème solaire*
dinner	*dîner*		**swimming**	*nager*
father	*père*		**taxi**	*taxi*
French fries	*frites*		**tent**	*tente*
hamburger	*steak hâché*		**I'm thirsty**	*j'ai soif*
hot	*chaud*		**tomato**	*tomate*
hotel	*hôtel*		**towel**	*serviette de bain*
			train	*train*
			train station	*gare*
			water	*eau*

≥ FRENCH WORDS ≥

Write down any other words that you see.
Add the English if you know it, or ask an adult
to help you work out what each word means:

WORD JUMBLE

Below are some French words that you'll find in this activity book, but they're all mixed up! Can you unscramble them and work out what they mean?

Here's an example for you (I've helped you out a bit by putting the first letter in capitals):

crMei

French
Merci

English
Thank you

eGra

French

English

jBoruno

French

English

usJ

French

English

rèFer

French

English

inV

French

English

nobBons

French

English

iutH

French

English

niPa

French

English

SPORTS

Lots of people come to France to play sport. Some compete seriously in the Tour de France bicycle race, the French Tennis Open or the Le Mans car races, and some just to have fun skiing in the winter.

Tennis

Tennis is probably a French game. Around the 12th century young French priests started playing a game of handball. This was called *le jeu de paume* (palm game). This may have hurt their hands so they started wearing gloves, then they had gloves with strings across them and eventually rackets.

FACT:
If you want to impress a French person, tell them what a good year 1998 was – it was the year France won the football World Cup.

Tour de France

This is a big bicycle race in very tight clothes that goes on for almost three weeks. Some bizarre facts for the average rider:

1. **He burns 123,900 calories during the race and**
2. **Wears out three bicycle chains**

The Olympics

It was a French man, Baron Pierre de Coubertin (1863–1937) who in 1894 came up with the modern idea of the Olympic Games.

SPORTS DIARY

Make a note here of all the sports you did on holiday, like swimming, skiing, walking and cycling:

ACTIVITY DIARY

Make a list here of the books and comics that you took to read on holiday:

Writing postcards

Postcards are a nice way of telling people at home a little bit about your holiday. You can send them to your friends, grandparents or other family members. You could even send one to yourself for when you get home!

Mont Saint-Michel

Postcard games

A French novel called *La Disparition* does not contain a single letter E. Why not try writing a postcard home like that?

Anyone can buy a postcard with a nice view. Why not have a family competition to see who can find the worst postcard for the holiday?

FOOD

French food is famous all over the world. Eating is very important to the French and they like to take a long time over meals.

Petit déjeuner **(breakfast):** it means 'little lunch' so don't expect a big fry-up. You can often choose from croissants, cheese, ham, fruit and pastries.

Déjeuner **(lunch):** lunch is important and lots of shops and businesses close for two hours or more in the middle of the day.

Dîner **(dinner):** don't be surprised to see a dog in even the poshest restaurant. He probably won't have a seat at the table but the French do like to take their pooches with them.

Cheese (*Fromage*)

The average French person eats over 20 kilos of cheese per year. If you like cheese then you are in luck as there are about 500 different kinds. Each area makes its own so try something local.

Roquefort cheese: made from sheep's milk. The French call it the King of Cheeses.

Camembert: made from cow's milk. There are three different kinds but they all come from Normandy.

Brie: made from sheep and goat's milk in the Île-de-France, which is the region around Paris.

What is the name of the cheese made in the place you are staying?

Garlic (Ail)

French people like to put lots of garlic in their food. Vampires beware!

CURIOUS CHEESE FACT: Comté cheese is best eaten 30 months after it is made.

French Fries or Chips (*Frites*)

Chips is the French word for crisps, and the French word for chips is *frites*. So make sure you order the correct thing! Both France and Belgium claim that they invented 'French fries' and we wouldn't want to start a fight. Belgians say that their street vendors sold these 'Belgian fries' from pushcarts long before the French thought it was a good idea. The Americans didn't have fries until the 1880s.

Wine (*Vin*) – for grown-ups only!

French wine is famous worldwide, especially Champagne, which is named after the region in France where it is made. France now makes one-fifth of all the wine made in the world.

Bread (*Pain*)

Bread is a very big part of the French diet. French bread contains no fat so it becomes stale very quickly. This is why people visit the bakery (*boulangerie*) at least once a day.

Mustard (*Moutarde*)

The town of Dijon is famous for its mustard. Mustard is very hot, so taste a very small amount first if you want to try it.

FUN FACT:
You can squish a cork down to half its size and within hours it will be back to normal.

Desserts

Beignets: French doughnuts eaten especially during Mardi Gras (Shrove Tuesday). The doughnuts are deep-fried, served covered in powered sugar and not good for diets.

Crème brûlée: custard with caramelized sugar topping

Crêpe: very thin pancake. They can be eaten all year but especially on 2 February (Fête de la Chandeleur) when the round, yellow pancakes are said to represent light.

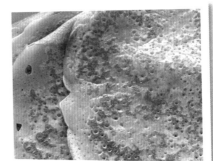

Glace: ice cream

   fraise – strawberry flavour

   au chocolat – chocolate

   à la vanille – vanilla (sometimes it's just too easy)

Mousse au chocolat: chocolate mousse

Tarte aux fraises: strawberry tart

Tarte aux pommes: apple tart

Monsieur Mangetout (Mr Eat-it-all)

If anyone in your family has a big or an odd appetite then you should compare them to a French man named Monsieur Mangetout. He is actually a man from Grenoble called Michel Lotito. Mangetout is well named because he has eaten things that the rest of us wouldn't even want on the menu, including:

- **18 bicycles**
- **1 computer**
- **7 televisions**
- **2 beds**
- **1 small aeroplane (Cessna 150)**
- **15 shopping trolleys**
- **6 chandeliers**
- **1 pair of skis**

The plane was taken apart, cut up, and he then spent two years (1978–1980) eating it. Mangetout started eating odd things when he was a kid. He was born with especially thick stomach and intestine walls and has very strong stomach acid. He says his meals, washed down with mineral oil and water, never give him any trouble but that bananas and hard-boiled eggs make him sick. Between 1959 and 1996 Mangetout ate nine tons of metal.

WHAT'S ON THE MENU?

See if you can spot any of these things on a menu:

Canard .... **Duck**

Confit .... **Meat preserved in its own fat**

Coq au vin .... **Chicken stewed in red wine sauce**

Coquilles Saint-Jacques .... **Sea scallops**

Cuisses de grenouille .... **Frog's legs**
(very skinny, taste a bit like chicken)

Escargots .... **Snails**

Florentine .... **'with spinach'**

Gâteau .... **Cake**

Gratiné .... **'with toasted cheese or crumb topping'**

Jambon .... **Usually ham but can also be a shoulder of pork**

Moules .... **Mussels**

Pâté .... **Meat spread**

Profiteroles .... **Pastries filled with cream**

Salade .... **Salad**

Soupe à l'oignon gratinée .... **French onion soup**

Steak Tartare .... **Chopped raw meat with egg, onion, parsley and capers. Do not ask for this to be served hot!**

Tournedos .... **Beef fillet**

Abats
You may not want these. The British call it offal and it's the bits of meat like brain, heart, liver, kidneys, tongue or cow's stomach that are not top of everyone's list.

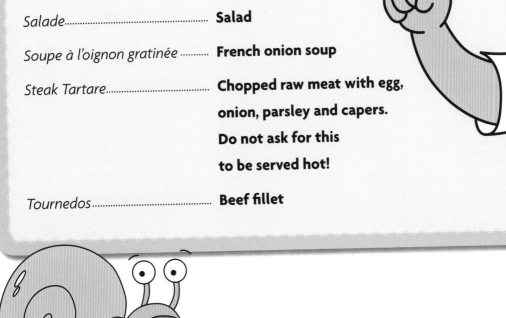

MY FOOD DIARY

The yummiest things I ate in France were:

The most disgusting things I ate in France were:

With my meals I like to drink:

Ask an adult for the receipt for one of your meals and stick it here:

HAPPY HOLIDAY

Travel journalists get to go all over the world to try out lots of places, hotels, food and things to do so they can help us decide where to go on holiday. While you're on the way home, why don't you pretend you're a reporter and write a review of your time in France? You'll need to say what was good and bad, what you most enjoyed and what you least enjoyed. It might be helpful to get some suggestions from everybody else travelling with you in case you've forgotten anything.

Happy Holidays!

Answers

Page 11 (Spot the Difference)

1. Sandi is tucking in her napkin.
2. French man has appeared.
3. Sign has appeared on door.
4. Baguettes in window.
5. Café sign has disappeared.
6. Wheel has been replaced with flower.
7. Snail has appeared.
8. Flower pot has gone.
9. Pigeon on the awning has disappeared.
10. Light on car is missing.

Page 18 (Counting in French)

Deux	Un	Six
Cinq	Quatre	Trois

Page 23 (Word Jumble)

2. French: Gare
   English: Train Station
3. French: Bonjour
   English: Hello
4. French: Jus
   English: Juice
5. French: Frère
   English: Brother
6. French: Vin
   English: Wine
7. French: Bonbons
   English: Sweets
8. French: Huit
   English: Eight
9. French: Pain
   English: Bread

Sandi Toksvig's
TRAVEL GUIDE TO FRANCE

A RED FOX BOOK 978 1 862 30431 4

First published in Great Britain by Red Fox, an imprint of Random House Children's Books
A Random House Group Company

This edition published 2009

1 3 5 7 9 10 8 6 4 2

Text copyright © Sandi Toksvig, 2009   Illustrations copyright © Dynamo, 2009   Design by Dynamo

The right of Sandi Toksvig to be identified as the author of this work has been
asserted in accordance with the Copyright, Designs and Patents Act 1988.

Red Fox Books are published by Random House Children's Books, 61–63 Uxbridge Road, London W5 5SA

www.kidsatrandomhouse.co.uk   www.rbooks.co.uk

Addresses for companies within The Random House Group Limited can be found at:
www.randomhouse.co.uk/offices.htm

THE RANDOM HOUSE GROUP Limited Reg. No. 954009

A CIP catalogue record for this book is available from the British Library.

Printed and bound in China

Photography: ©Shutterstock

Stephanie Strathdee, Mumbo Jumbo, Peter Baxter, Knud Nielson, SnowWons, Tayana Boyko, Clara Natoli, Villedieu
Christophe, Alfred Wekelo, Jakez, Tomo Jesenicnik, Kmitu, Martin Nemec, Djordje Zoric, Loulouphotos, Jakez, Erickn, Pepita.